BRITAIN IN OLD PHOTOGRAPHS

THE LANCASHIRE COAST

CATHERINE ROTHWELL

ALAN SUTTON PUBLISHING LIMITED

Alan Sutton Publishing Limited
Phoenix Mill · Far Thrupp · Stroud
Gloucestershire · GL5 2BU

First published 1995

Copyright © Catherine Rothwell, 1995

Cover photograph: (front) the Stella Marie,
1941; (back) Bertha Wyatt, 1901.

British Library Cataloguing in Publication Data.
A catalogue record for this book is available from
the British Library.

ISBN 0–7509–0984–6

Typeset in 9/10 Sabon.
Typesetting and origination by
Alan Sutton Publishing Limited.
Printed in Great Britain by
WBC Ltd, Bridgend.

Contents

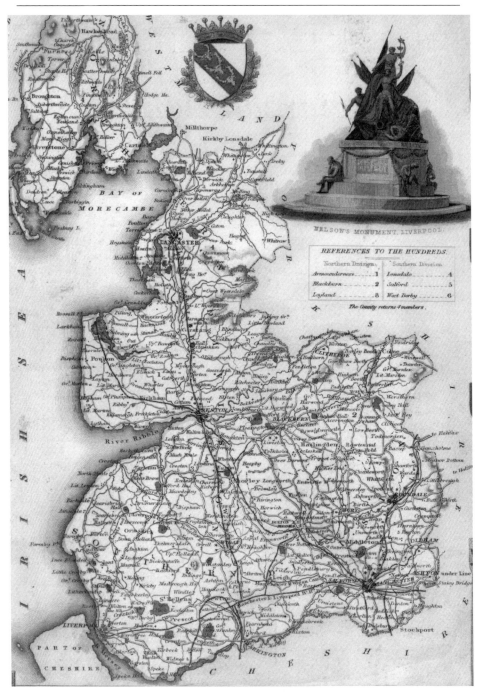

Map of Lancashire, 1828.

Introduction

The Lancashire Coast is surely one of the most interesting stretches of coastline in the whole country, a fact illustrated by old photographs which highlight such a richness of variety. For wrecks and ruggedness the palm must go to Cornwall, but for sheer diversity Lancashire can have few rivals. The possession of the largest bay, Morecambe Bay, with Liverpool Bay an interesting second, adds to that reputation.

Winds soar to gale force, whipping up mountainous seas and driving them inland, sinking ships and breaching sea defences, even swallowing up villages. In 1844 a poor labourer, William Bates, was blown 'off a precipice'; at such times the Lancashire saying was 'Boreas is on the bluster'. The death-toll was high over 100 years ago when fishing and cockling were the main livelihoods. On such dire occasions as Black Friday in 1894, Liverpool, Lytham, Southport, Fleetwood and Cartmel paid the price in lives. Often more than one member of the family was snatched by the cruel sea as those brave men, splendid sailors as they were, volunteered to man the lifeboats when the need arose.

Even in modern times the sea takes its toll. The storm surge of water, which carried the *King Orry IV* away from her moorings at Glasson to leave her stranded on Thurnham Marsh until the next spring tides, also broke adrift the supertanker *Myrina* from Tranmere Oil Terminal and cast her on to Packington Bank (so designated on old maps) where she broke her back. Another casualty of that wild night, 2 January 1976, with the tidal surge 6 ft above datum, was the Liverpool Ferry Stage which sank.

Yet this devastating neighbour is both friend and foe. When the sea-bathing craze hit Britain the Lancashire coast, with golden sands, little inlets, sand dunes and gently shelving beaches proved ideal. From shallow seas and flat shores in the south to cliffs and grander vistas at the northern end the most fastidious visitors could find something to their liking.

Once the railway arrived, linking central and east Lancashire directly with coastal towns from Liverpool to Barrow, there was no holding back development. Interspersed with the new resorts were many small but useful ports supporting a coastal cargo trade. It is interesting to note that the shipping line Coast Lines of Liverpool had a fine ship called the *Lancashire Coast*. With 100 ships at one time they traded around the coasts of Britain.

Mighty Liverpool, unique in the splendour of its buildings, from St George's Hall to the then-futuristic iron and glass offices of the 1860s in Water and Cork Streets, logged 4,411 vessels in 1862. Less well known is the fact that Lancaster, at its busiest, shipped more cargoes than any port except London, Liverpool and Bristol: exotic Madeira wines, cocoa, lime juice, ginger, oranges, lemons, hogsheads of sugar, puncheons of rum, casks of coffee, bales of cotton. At Lancaster as at Preston and Poulton, vessels were also engaged in the notorious trade in black ivory – as the slave trade was described. Ships' captains bargained with the King of Calabar to receive men in exchange for bright cotton cloth, trinkets and utensils. *Swallow*, built at Lancaster, was advertised as 'of proper dimensions for the slave trade'.

Silting was a problem which bedevilled many a small Lancashire port and led to the transfer of Lancaster's shipping to Glasson. This port had the first dock to be fitted with special lock gates enabling vessels to remain on an even keel.

Attached to the myriad small ports were shipbuilding yards humming with activity. When trade slackened at one, men would walk miles down the coast to the next, carrying their tools and carrying also, in their minds, the blueprints of construction. Actual plans did not always exist.

The charting of the coast, especially Liverpool Bay and the approaches to Port Fleetwood, was carried out efficiently by Captain Henry Mangles Denham in the late 1830s. Morecambe Bay was surveyed by Staff Commander John Richards in 1871 and re-sounded in 1953. This was of vital importance as Bernard's Wharf, Shell Wharf, Sunderland Shoulder, Salters and the Horse Bank had been death traps for ships.

The short cut to the Furness peninsula, 9 miles across Morecambe Bay, was highly dangerous. It was traversed by the Romans and the Quakers and the swift-running tides claimed 'many a man and his mare'. The crossing of this ancient coach road is safe only three hours before and three hours after high tide and even then only with an experienced guide. When returning from Silverdale, Thomas Buxton's coach blew over in a gale in March 1850. He had to abandon it and the next tide cast up the wreckage; there were even less happy instances of the entire cart and horse disappearing into the quicksands.

Ancient Heysham, before it became a boom town, had many farms, market gardens and strawberry gardens supplying the hordes of visitors that needed feeding. Lancashire gained a great reputation for keeping a good table, for excellent value for money, and for golden-hearted landladies who became friends for life, especially at Blackpool and Morecambe, where visitors returned year after year. Affectionately remembered are the pleasure steamers of Southport, Morecambe, Lytham, Fleetwood and Blackpool: *Belle, Bickerstaffe, Greyhound, Deerhound, Lady Margaret, Wellington, Queen of the Bay, Cumbria*. The fast-sailing yacht *Fleetwood*, hired for summer seasons, was the one used by Captain Denham and Lieutenant Williams for the government surveys. Thousands recall the Isle of Man Steam Packet Company ships, which served the Lancashire ports of Liverpool, Fleetwood and Heysham, and the majestic Royal Mail boats to Ireland – in their heyday, akin to liners.

'Beauty surrounds, health abounds' was Morecambe's motto, and 'The sun goes down splendidly beyond the Irish Sea, all Lakeland catches the glow' wrote one visitor expressing for many the fame of coastal sunsets. *The Lancashire Coast in Old Photographs* will bring back memories of carefree holidays: sailing, sand-yachting, swimming, paddling, castle-building and, as the sun went down, convivial company around groaning tables. White-washed thatched cottages, tea shops, wagonettes, charabancs and grandmother's ankle-length skirts are all to be found in 208 old photographs calling back memorable yesterdays.

LIVERPOOL TO SOUTHPORT

Promenade and pier, Southport, 1909.

Oceanic, Liverpool, *c.* 1900. There were two ships named *Oceanic*, in 1871–96 and 1899–1916. This is T.H. Ismay's pioneer steamer, White Star Liner and Royal Mail Ship. Note the paddle steamer in the background. The best known and fastest of the White Star ships was *Hoghton Tower*. She left Liverpool on 26 June 1869 with seventy passengers on her maiden voyage, captained by Digby Murray, and arrived in Melbourne on 7 September. The fame of Liverpool had spread across the world. The *Illustrated London News*, in January 1864, reported: 'Captain Edward G. Lott of the steamer *Persia* was honoured with entertainment on the 11th inst at Delmonica's, 5th Avenue, New York previous to his 300th passage across the ocean.'

In 1900 one of the most wonderful sights in the world could be seen from the top of the Liver Building: 4 miles of quays with their giant liners, paddle and tramp steamers; colourful house flags; Gladstone Docks, the largest in the world and containing the largest tobacco warehouse in the world; shipyards; 700 warehouses capable of holding two million bales of cotton; the headquarters of the Liverpool Cotton Association. A Liverpool Docks broadsheet of 1836 listed destinations all over the world. Famous shipping companies using the port in the 1950s included Cunard White Star, Canadian Pacific, Blue Funnel, Royal Mail and Ellerman.

Mrs Adolphus, *c.* 1840. She sailed to India in the 1840s when Liverpool port charges were '1/6*d* per ton for sago inwards, cotton from India twopence for 100 lbs, oranges and lemons twopence per cask, tar three halfpence per barrel'. She took a large wardrobe of clothes, furniture and cooking pots supplied by a firm that advertised in the *Daily Graphic* especially for this purpose.

The tariff at the massive White Adelphi Hotel, where passengers stayed before boarding the Duchess liners, sounded modest in the 1920s: a single room with private bath 15*s* 6*d*; luncheon in the Grill Room 4*s* 6*d*. Charles Dickens, when he stayed, praised the Adelphi, which could boast marble bathrooms, Turkish baths and swimming pools.

A prosperous Liverpool lady, 1870. Photographed by Vanderbilt of 10 James Street, enlargements were obtainable in oil, water colours or crayons. Liverpool society was well-to-do. Its city held Lewis's first multiple store in Ranelagh Street; the Fabian Society (first outside London); the first steel-hulled ship, built in 1864 by Liverpool-based Jones, Quigg and Company. Influential merchants like William Brown, who became Liverpool's MP, made fortunes but ploughed back their wealth into a truly great city of which they were justly proud.

In the 1860s vessels entering the port numbered 269,742. Calcutta jute clippers, tea and wool clippers, with their different nationalities and houseflags, added to the colourful scene on the waterfront.

Commutation Row in William Brown Street, Liverpool, 1906. The Walker Art Gallery, Public Library and Merseyside County Museum are among the fine buildings shown. St George's Hall is round the corner in Lime Street. The 150-ft high Wellington Monument is topped by a statue cast from cannon captured at the Battle of Waterloo.

South Road, Waterloo, 1930s. Boots the chemist is on the left. The sandy beach, with its safe bathing area, was a popular place for watching the shipping. Crosby grew out of the district of Waterloo and was where wealthy Liverpool merchants built their Regency houses.

White Star Australian Packets operated between Liverpool and Melbourne from the 1860s. When passage through the Suez Canal became available in November 1869 Smiths, shipbuilders, signed contracts for four steamers and built only two more sailing ships. The fastest of the 'Cities' was *City of Perth*, built by Connells in 1868. *City of Benares*, *Madras*, *Madrid* and *Glasgow*, famous on the New Zealand run, were also steaming east at about the same time as another shipbuilders, Brocklebank's, equally beautiful vessels: *Alexandra*, *Candabar* and *Tenasserin*, built in the 1860s by Harland and Wolff.

The Allan and Dominion Lines were transporting emigrants from Liverpool at special low rates: 'Assisted ocean rates for agricultural labourers, their families, female domestics, at £3 per adult, mechanics, general labourers and their families, infants under one year 10/-.'

The mayor's house, a former Dale Street inn, Liverpool. Acquired in 1515 it became the site of the first town hall. In November 1561, when havoc was wreaked on the harbour in an epic storm, the mayor marched all able-bodied men, rich and poor, to the scene of the harbour's destruction and ordered them to rebuild it. A later grand town hall, now Liverpool's oldest building, was designed by John Wood of Bath and built in 1749–54. The dome, added in 1795, is crowned with a figure of Minerva designed by C.F. Rossi. The original town hall had its thatch replaced by slates in the sixteenth century when it also served as a custom house.

The Prince's Landing Stage, 1900. Opened on 1 September 1857, it made the embarkation of passengers safer and easier. Before that, John Waterworth, the Isle of Man Steam Packet Company's boatman, used to row passengers between steamers and the floating bridge. He died in 1868.

William Brown Street, Liverpool, 1906. It was named after Sir William Brown MP. Among the magnificent buildings are the Brown Library, designed by Thomas Allom, built in Corinthian style, and opened in 1860. Extensive bomb damage was inflicted in May 1941 but the ground floor was restored, by 1945, to house a fresh stock of books for the Central Lending Library.

The Old Lake, Wavertree, 1918. It was one of many fine parks constructed in or near Liverpool. Stanley Park, as attractive as Sefton, already had a popular aviary in 1918. Newsham Park, reached by West Derby or London Road, was created from the Newsham estates.

St George's Hall, 1902. Designed by the young architect Harvey Lonsdale Elmes, the hall was built opposite Liverpool Lime Street station. It opened in 1854 and cost £333,000 including fittings. The pediment contains C.R. Cockerell's design in Caen stone representing commerce and arts in relation to Britannia, then at the height of her powers.

Lord Clive, c. 1880, an iron ship built by T. and J. Brocklebank, who also built *Alexandra, Belfast* and *Majestic* (see page 11). J.P. Corry and Company built the 'Stars': *Star of Persia, Greece, Bengal.* Between 1863 and 1887, twenty-two R. and J. Craig's 'Counties' were launched: 1,000-ton ships which made Liverpool to Calcutta in ninety days. From 1866 to 1882 seventeen 'Cities' were produced for Smiths, including *City of Benares* (see page 11).

The clippers of the 1870s included the large fleet of East India traders owned by the British Shipowners' Company under its managing director James Beazley. They had sixteen iron ships, the pioneer ships of the line being *British Prince* and *British Princess* built by Clover of Birkenhead. The famous Captain Cobb took the iron clipper *Nelson,* fully laden with troops and passengers, to New Zealand, but the shrewd shipmaster did not approve of the sail plan of either *Nelson* or *Victory* so, for the next voyage, had it altered to single topgallant sails and double topsails with the addition of royals. Dismissed for making the change without authorisation, he was offered the fine ship *Sir Jansetjee Family* which he commanded until his death, from drowning, in Manila.

The first office in Liverpool of the Isle of Man Steam Packet Company, *c.* 1882. On the right is Jane Riley's Dining Rooms, on the left a sail maker's, the Liverpool Screw Towing Company and the Liverpool Lighterage Company (agents James Newton and Company). Founded in 1830, the Isle of Man Steam Packet Company was a remarkable undertaking, 'its record unmatched in the whole of shipping industry' (Liverpool *Daily Post*). Before 1832 it was known as the Mona's Isle Company after which the first steamer, launched on 30 June 1830, was named. She could complete the voyage between Liverpool and Douglas in eight hours. Robert Napier, who designed her engines, considered her fast for her day. Her popularity was reflected in the making of Liverpool transfer-ware jugs bearing the ship's image and the legend 'Success to the *Mona's Isle*'. *Mona's Isle II*, later renamed *Ellan Vannin*, was built in 1860 and *Mona's Isle III* in 1882.

John Aindow, Formby lifeboatman, *c.* 1892. His family did sterling service, rescuing many a casualty off the Liverpool–Formby–Crosby coast. Bob, John, Tom, Joseph, William, Jack and Charles all served.

The Revd Richard Formby (1760–1832), a Lord of the Manor and first incumbent of St John's Liverpool (near where St George's Hall now stands), was made a Freeman of the City of Liverpool for the great work he did towards saving the shipwrecked. The Formby lifeboat station, destroyed by tempest, was rebuilt in 1809 and a boat supplied from Liverpool. Of many storms, that of 1814 was most severe. Bold Fleetwood Hesketh wrote to his cousin, the Revd Richard Formby of Formby: 'I suffered very severely by the late storms. My fleet is all blown up on Cartmel sands.'

London Road, Liverpool, 1900. Moore's Dining Rooms is on the corner of Lime Street next to the Legs of Man inn (right). Vintage tram 173 clangs down the busy thoroughfare at ten to three in the afternoon.

Duke of Northumberland lifeboat trials, Albert Dock, Liverpool, *c.* 1880. The church in the background on the left is that of St Nicholas, the sailors' church. During its long history it has housed prisoners of war (in 1644) and been grievously bombed (in 1940).

Viking in dry dock, Douglas, Isle of Man, 1930. Built in 1905 by Cammell Laird, and a familiar sight off the Lancashire coast, she primarily served Fleetwood, becoming an institution in the town. From 1915 to 1919 she functioned as HMS *Vindex*, sea-plane carrier. A veritable giant, she was 361 ft long, 42 ft broad and had four decks; she was registered to carry 1,950 passengers. The largest and fastest of the Isle of Man Steam Packet Company's fleet, her record passage was two hours twenty-two minutes from Douglas Head to Fleetwood at an average speed of 23.2 knots. *Viking* arrived with the punctuality of a railway train and carried 170,000 passengers in one season alone. She was broken up in 1954 and her ship's bell preserved at Fleetwood.

Opening ceremony for the Queensway Tunnel, 1934. Opened by King George V and Queen Mary, the Queensway was the first Mersey road tunnel between Liverpool and Birkenhead. Nearly 2 miles long, it was, at that time, the world's longest underwater tunnel. The Kingsway Tunnel linking Liverpool and Wallesey was opened almost forty years later in 1971. Crossing to Birkenhead, under the River Mersey, Queensway was an impressive engineering feat. The architect who drafted the plan, in 1922, was Herbert J. Rowse and the engineer in charge of this £7 million undertaking was B.H.M. Hewett. Because of the huge number of vehicles propelled by internal combustion engines the ventilating system had to be highly effective. Two and a half million cubic feet of air every minute was brought along the kerbs. On each side of the river three ventilation stations with large towers were built.

Liverpool Anglican Cathedral, 1940. Originally intended to be larger than St Peter's in Rome, the cathedral took 75 years to build, partly because of being interrupted by two world wars. Edward VII laid the foundation stone in 1904. This solid, sandstone construction, with its central tower 331 ft high spanning the entire width, was designed by Sir Giles Gilbert Scott.

Liverpool Philharmonic Hall, 1939. Noted for its art deco bas relief designs, it is now being refurbished. In 1840, when the first Cunard passenger liner sailed from Liverpool to America, the Philharmonic Society was formed by a group of amateur musicians. The first principal conductor was Zeugheer Herrmann and the first Philharmonic Hall was opened on 27 August 1849 amidst great festivity.

A tug off the Lancashire coast assists two sailing vessels to port, 1900. Records show that the ship *Nicteaux*, carrying cotton from New Brunswick to Liverpool, struck on Ted's Bank but refloated with all crew safe.

Fleetwood-on-Wyre. The lithograph is by Liverpool artist Gavin Herdman. In the late 1820s the Lancashire coast buzzed with speculation regarding a much-needed port and harbour of refuge. With the financial backing of the Lord of the Manor, Fleetwood was chosen above rival claimants.

Formby lifeboat, *John and Henrietta*, 1892. Two horses dragged the boat to the water's edge from the lifeboat house, seen here with its new frontage. The first lifeboat station on this stretch of coast was at Formby in 1776, but rescues were made long before.

Trinity Road, Bootle, July 1903. Bootle was once a fashionable seaside resort, like Crosby, but between 1824 and 1860 docks were built here. A few are still in use although many have become ship-breakers' yards.

Marine Lake, Southport, 1899. The lake stretched from the south end of the Promenade to opposite the convalescent hospital. Its southern part opened in 1887 and the northern in 1892. It was extremely popular for boating and yachting: rowing competitions, regattas and water carnivals were held.

The pier, Southport, 1905. There was a fine promenading area on this the country's longest pier. At the end of the pier the shrimping 'nobbies' tied up, many of them with Liverpool as port of provenance. Each day in the season the steamer *Wellington* called, and feeding the gulls from the pier head was quite a spectacle, watched by many from Thom's Tea House.

Shipwreck, Formby, 1898. Spectators thronged the shore on these occasions, hampering salvage work. In October of the same year the *Minnie*, carrying corn for Parkinson & Tomlinson, millers of Poulton-le-Fylde, was involved in collision with the *Duke of Cornwall* off the Lancashire Coast.

Southport shrimpers, 1920. Southport was famous for the quality of its shrimps and cockles. Rakes and riddles were used to collect them in baskets for transportation in carts. One firm, in the business for 100 years, closed in 1947 when supplies dwindled.

Windy Harbour Farmhouse, Hillside road, *c.* 1890. It was then 200 years old, one of Southport's oldest links with the past.

Churchtown Mill, *c.* 1920. The last of Southport's windmills, it was once one of many that ground corn into flour. At Crosby, on the main road between Southport and Liverpool, was a taller four-storey mill. Cotton and silk weaving were also carried on at Churchtown.

Mrs Moor's original home-potted shrimps and meat shop, 8 Neville Street, Southport, 1897. Famous customers included Lord Derby, Martin Harvey and Fred Terry. She also made treacle toffee, pickles and marmalade. It is thought that this successful business was started by a Quaker lady.

Another place famous for seafood was Broadbent's Oyster Bar on Coronation Street between the Buffalo Arms and a saddler's premises. It was popular for oysters and ale. If customers wished they could bring their own 'small beer' to wash down the oysters.

Emma Fielden, the author's maternal grandmother, 1913. Born in the 1850s Emma Fielden lived in Rossendale and used to visit Southport in preference to Blackpool, deeming the latter vulgar. Beautifully dressed, she is photographed on one of the carved chairs in her son-in-law's photographic studio. Mrs Fielding enjoyed strolling down Lord Street where the band played and the coloured fairy lights were lit amongst the trees. She thought the resort's shops and cafés most elegant and her hat may well have been bought in Southport. For summer wear she had a Bangkok straw trimmed with a bunch of shining red cherries that looked, to young eyes, good enough to eat.

Marine Park, Southport, 1902. The crowds indicate the growth and popularity of this fashionable seaside resort. By 1920 the New Marine Gardens were thronged with enormous crowds during the season. On East Bank Street, adjoining Lord Street, Thompson's Café served delicious ices, Bradleys were outfitters and clothiers, and Jeffs fruiterers.

Steamer *Belle* arriving at Southport pier, 1912. Regardless of the tide *Belle* and *Cumbria* were able to come alongside to take trippers to Lytham, Blackpool, Beaumaris, Llandudno and the Isle of Man.

J.A. Tatham of Tarleton delivering fruit, Southport Market, early 1900s. The beasts are chained between shafts and wear leather blinkers in keeping with the rest of their all-leather harness. The fruit is stored in wooden crates; grapes packed in cork and other commodities protected by straw. A voluminous tarpaulin covers the stack of boxes and crates in case of rain but there is little protection for the driver. In the coldest weather the horses had blankets thrown over their backs but icy conditions were especially hazardous. If a horse fell and broke its leg it invariably had to be shot on the spot.

Early days in Southport, *c.* 1844. With visitors in mind, J. Whitehead, toy dealer, J. Riding, flour dealer and N. Craven, draper had set up shops alongside the Scarisbrick Arms.

Betty Ball, *c.* 1900. Southport's oldest donkey driver, she started offering donkeys for hire on the shore around 1850. She wore a long apron and a man's cloth cap. Her donkeys are being inspected for any signs of ill-health or misuse.

Chapel Street, Southport, 1840. Viewed from Central station Christ Church is just visible on the right and East Bank Street, where the Independent chapel was built in 1863, is on the left. Victoria Buildings, Central Chambers, the Liberal Club and the market were built later on the sandhills.

Probably Little London inn, *c.* 1900. On maps of the coast dating back 200 years is marked the hamlet of Little London. In the 1850s the lane leading through sandhills to Little London became Mornington Road, Southport. Virginia Street was known as Gorsey Lane.

Fishing boats, north side of Southport Pier, *c.* 1900. They are mainly from the Marshside fishing industry. These men, noted for their support of the Temperance Movement, held meetings in 'Peter's Dick's workshop' until the Revd Charles Hesketh granted them land on which to build a Temperance Hall.

Haymaking, Hesketh Lane, Tarleton, *c.* 1880. No Sunshine Reaper and Binder or Massey-Harris Kicker here. Southport visitors demanded strawberries which were grown and picked not far from here at Douglas Bank.

IN THE YEAR OF OUR LORD
1792
THIS HOUSE WAS BUILT
IN MEMORY of D.W. SUTTON
of North-meols who was the
first Founder & Executor of
SouthPort which was call'd his
Folly for many Years, and it prove
that his foresight was his Wisdom
which should be remembred with
gratitude by the LORDS of this
Manor and the Inhabitants of this
PLACE ALSO

Memorial stone. It was erected to honour D.W. Sutton of North Meols who was regarded as the founder of Southport. His house, Duke's Folly, built in 1792, 'proved that his foresight was his wisdom'. Duke's Folly became the Royal Hotel. By the 1900s Southport was only half-an-hour's train ride from Liverpool. At the height of summer the Marine Lake, the pier, the Switchback and the old-fashioned Hobby Horses were patronised by adults while children loved paddling and digging in the sands. The Marine Drive was constructed in 1894 when North and South Marine Lakes were joined; this ended the days of sand yachting introduced as early as 1830.

Helter-skelter Lighthouse, Southport, 1910. Next to it is the Bicycle Railway. The Helter-skelter attracted hundreds of holidaymakers as did the one at Blackpool. Southport also had a water chute, airships and aerial railway, all part of a fairground opened in 1903 at the southern end of the Marine Lake. In the early 1900s Sir Hiram Maxim's flying machine, river caves and the figure-of-eight toboggan railway cost no more than 3*d* to visit or ride upon.

Lord Street, Southport, 1900. It was one of the country's most famous boulevards. At no. 37 T.R. Highton, complete house furnisher, sold quality furniture made by Waring & Gillow of Lancaster: 'rugs, mats, curtains, bedsteads and bedding'.

Lord Street, 1890s. Note the tram bound for Roe Lane. The white pinafores of the children, the long, white dresses of young ladies plus the men's straw boaters indicate a fine summer day, in spite of the all-year-round obligatory black of the older women.

Lord Street, early 1900s. Southport's splendid line of buildings along Lord Street numbered Christ Church, the Town Hall, Cambridge Hall, the Art Gallery and Bank Buildings.

North Promenade, 1900. 'Southport is the playground for all Lancashire', wrote a critic in 1902, unimpressed by the town but praising the belt of sandhills that stretched as far as Blundellsands. The Botanic Gardens, built on the site of the old Strawberry Gardens, also earned his praise.

Promenade and lake, Southport, 20 June 1920. Horse-drawn vehicles and hand carts were used to convey visitors and luggage, replacing the earlier donkey carts or shandries.

Aughton Road, Birkdale. Linked to Southport by tram, by 1866 Birkdale had become a separate borough. Its town hall was built in 1871. In the same year the Southport and Birkdale Club Co. Ltd was established on this road.

PRESTON TO

THORNTON-CLEVELEYS

Central Promenade, Blackpool, c. 1902.

Longton Marshes, 1900. Rabbits were regularly part of the diet. Lifeboatman William Bibby even caught pheasants in Southport's Lord Street area. The marshes from Hesketh Bank to Crossens were also rich in samphire. It grew in the silty soil at the sea's edge; country people gathered it in late September to make into a pickle.

Building Preston Docks, 1899. Because Lytham was inadequate as a port, hope was placed in Preston, a short run from the sea. Unfortunately the channel of the River Ribble proved treacherous and difficult to dredge.

The barque *Clara*. She was wrecked in December 1906 on her way from Norway to Preston, a trip she had made without mishap on twenty-four previous occasions. The 430-ton wooden barque was built in 1857 at Miramichi and was captained by Olaf Peterson. Carrying 56 tons of wooden deals, she had tried, without success, to obtain a pilot a mile south of the Nelson buoy. At midnight, in a heavy squall, her keel struck bottom. Under the continual bumping a portion of the rudder broke and her main topmast crashed down, carrying away the sails. With capsize imminent the crew took to the ship's boat, but were blown helplessly over treacherous sandbanks until landed by Fleetwood lifeboat at 8 a.m. Alerted by the lifeboat signal gun, hundreds had gathered on the Promenade to watch the drama.

Disaster overtook a similar barque of 545 tons more than 50 years before – the *Henrietta*, which sailed between Liverpool and the Nigerian slave trade port of Bonny. Her captain, Niels Peter Jacobson, born in 1815 the son of a Danish sea captain, was paid £15 a month by Lovatt & Corran of Liverpool. The *Henrietta* had gone to help the *Laura Campbell* which had lost her main mast and sails in a December gale. According to the Liverpool *Telegraph and Shipping Gazette*, wreckage and letters from the *Henrietta* were washed up some weeks after the incident in January 1851. Captain Jacobson and his crew were presumed lost at sea.

The offices of the *Preston Guardian* and *Lancashire Daily Post*, pre-1914. Pony traps, like the one in front of the building, cantered all over town delivering the papers. Early trains took the news to Blackpool, Lytham and Southport, towns which had set up their own newspapers in the 1840s: the *Southport Visiter* and the *Fleetwood Chronicle*. Next door to the Guardian office at 124 Fishergate is Cowan & Sons Spectacle Specialists, with their large eye-glasses sign on the window above.

G.R. and J. Pemberton's paper boys, Preston, 1905. They stand outside the premises beneath posters advertising 'Football Competition 79 . . . free paper patterns given away in the magazine *Domestic Life*'. An article on 'What does it cost to be Lord Mayor?' would seem to indicate that Preston Guild was under discussion, an important civic occasion held every twenty years in 'Proud Preston'. The *Sunday Times* then cost a penny. Also on offer were *Racing Tips* and 112 columns in *The People*. Emile Zola's play *Paris*, which had set even France by the ears, was due to be performed in the town. Pemberton's has been delivering newspapers since 1872.

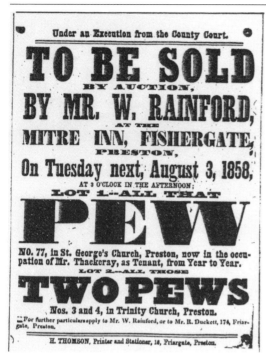

Under an Execution from the County Court.

TO BE SOLD

BY AUCTION,

BY MR. W. RAINFORD,

AT THE

MITRE INN, FISHERGATE,

PRESTON,

On Tuesday next, August 3, 1858,

AT 3 O'CLOCK IN THE AFTERNOON;

LOT 1—ALL THAT

PEW

NO. 77, in St. George's Church, Preston, now in the occupation of Mr. Thackeray, as Tenant, from Year to Year.

LOT 2—ALL THOSE

TWO PEWS

Nos. 3 and 4, in Trinity Church, Preston.

☞For further particulars apply to Mr. W. Rainford, or to Mr. R. Duckett, 174, Friargate, Preston.

H. THOMSON, Printer and Stationer, 16, Friargate, Preston.

Sale of church pews, Preston, 1858. Erected in 1723, St George's Church was restored in 1844. Of 800 sittings only eighty were free and churchwardens valued the income from pew rent. William Rainford, the auctioneer, had premises at 174 Friargate.

New Town Hall, Preston, 1863. This picture was presented with the *Preston Herald* on 6 September 1863. The foundation stone of the new town hall was laid by Robert Townley Parker, Guild Mayor, 'with all the Masonic Ceremony'. A town of Saxon antiquity, Preston was proud to consider itself as centre of the county of Lancashire and occupying a commanding position on the Ribble estuary. Among other fine buildings were the Philosophical Institution, St Peter's Church, the grammar school, the Institution for the Diffusion of Knowledge and St Walburgh's Church. There were fine streets and parades such as Stephenson Terrace, Avenham Walks and Winckley Square. This last contained the imposing residence of William Ainsworth. Many of these nineteenth-century buildings grew from the wealth of the cotton merchants. Messrs Horrockses, Miller & Company and Messrs Swainson, Birley & Company built huge cotton mills in the town.

Royal Field Artillery soldiers, Preston station, 1914. The loading gauge, hanging from the gantry and looking rather like a gallows, gave the safety limit for height and width of goods loaded into the wagons. In the mid-nineteenth century Preston had as many as five stations which were used by a number of small local companies. Eventually they amalgamated and used the North Union station on the south side of Fishergate. The original station had only two platforms and, although extra tracks and platforms were added, this was inadequate. Improvements were thwarted by acrimony between rival companies. Eventually the narrow tunnel under Fishergate was replaced by a large bridge over eight tracks and island platforms were built under a high iron and glass roof. By 1880 a new main entrance from Fishergate bridge had been opened and, with further additions and extensions, Preston, midway between Euston and Glasgow, became a major interchange station.

Tram no. 22, Preston, 1904. The electric tram car was made by the United Electric Car Company, Strand Road, who built thirty cars for service in Preston. This car held forty-eight passengers and, in 1907, was the first to be fitted with a top cover. The heavy snowfall of January 1910 meant that tram cars were stranded all over Preston.

River Ribble, Broadgate, Preston, 1921. When high tides occurred the Ribble overflowed its banks and flooded streets and playing fields. Centuries earlier, boats were swept out to sea from the boat-building yards when the tide tore over Ribble Banks.

The Grotto, St Anne's-on-Sea, 1929. It was completed as part of the promenade gardens on 9 June 1909 by local man Henry Gregson of Grove Cottage.

The boating pool and pier, St Anne's-on-Sea, *c.* 1930. The pier was opened in 1885, and by the early 1900s the new Moorish Pavilion had become known for its excellent musical concerts.

Mary Hawthornthwaite, *c.* 1902. Known as 'Aunt Cissie', she was sister to Robert who became miller at Thornton's Marsh Mill, where corn was ground.

The United Reformed White Church, Fairhaven, *c.* 1960. Built in Byzantine architectural style in 1912, it remains a notable landmark on the Lancashire coast. One of its founding members designed the stained-glass windows covering biblical subjects, for which it is locally famed.

Engraving of Blackpool's coast, 1784. Left to right: a spring well, Mrs Bailey's bath house, packing ground, bowling green, Mr Bailey's tavern, alcove, Mr Forshaw's tavern, Mr Crooke's post office, Mrs Hodson's tavern, Mr Hull's tavern, Mr Bonney's wine house, Mr Bonney's bath house, Mr Elson's, an ancient building, the public walk in front of these properties and (in the sea) two bathing machines. Printed by Sears Brothers, this westerly view of Blackpool appeared in Preston newspapers. The long line of cliffs is noteworthy. 'Packing ground' probably referred to pack horses and the supplies brought in to serve the early lodging houses.

The village of Blackpool stretched in a straight line parallel to the sea, above a range of cliffs which rose at one point to 100 ft above sea level. It was reported, in 1837, that on fine evenings the Isle of Man, 60 miles away, could be seen from the village. Virtually the whole of the Lancashire coast was visible: in one direction Heysham, Cockersand, Lancaster, Sunderland, Piel, Walney and Furness; in the other Thornton, Bispham, Poulton, Singleton, Lytham, Southport, the smoke of Liverpool and the chimneys of Preston. By that year Simpson's Hotel had been built on the edge of the Hawes. In the Moss, where sand drifts collected, relics from past ages were found embedded in peat: an antique cheese vat, two stone hand-mills, a brass axe and dagger, silver coins, shoes and wheels of a type unknown within memory of the traditions of the neighbourhood. Trunks of trees – alder, ash, oak, willow, sycamore – were also discovered in the Moss and a Dr Alderson declared: 'There was a subterranean forest extending all the way along the coast from the Ribble near Preston to the Mersey at Liverpool.'

North Shore, Blackpool, 1796. Cliff sites were obvious points to take advantage of the winds and erect windmills. Natural hazards proved too much, however, as gales destroyed sails and the encroaching sea washed away structures built on the shore. This was the fate of both Lytham lighthouse and Rossall windmill.

Ceremony to lay a foundation stone, Blackpool, 25 September 1891. In Blackpool buildings were burgeoning, but this was a 'special'. Here the foundation stone for Blackpool Tower is laid by the MP Sir Matthew White-Ridley.

Foudroyant, Blackpool, 1898. Wrecked off the North Pier on 16 June 1897 these are the sad remains of Lord Nelson's flagship the *Foudroyant*. This occasion was a classic example of the savagery of the Irish Sea in north-westerly gale conditions which, over the years, strewed the Fylde coast with wrecks. Summer storms proved no whit less violent than winter: another devastating flooding and wrecking occurred in June 1833 from which Peter Hesketh's Rossall estates never fully recovered.

G.Wheatley Cobb had restored and refitted the *Foudroyant* to be a show ship, at a cost of £20,000. After a short spell at Southport she was taken to Blackpool. Although warned that he would be in difficulties if the wind rose, Captain William John Robins was quite confident. *Foudroyant* broke from her moorings and was carried helplessly by the force of the storm. From the Wellington Hotel, Blackpool, Wheatley Cobb wrote to his mother at Caldicott Castle: 'We went back to the ship, and her condition is horrifying . . . huge, old timbers ripped in every direction, every internal fitting and bulkhead swept away and the decks rent to pieces.' Souvenirs were made from the timbers: walking sticks, jewel boxes, tables and other furniture. The copper was struck into medallions.

Sirene, 8 October 1892. She was a Norwegian barque of 666 tons. A violent storm had kept most vessels in port but *Sirene* set off from Fleetwood bound for Georgia, USA. She managed to get as far as Llandudno but, from that point, was blown steadily back until she foundered against the North Pier at Blackpool. The sea ran so high that the lifeboat could not put out and onlookers in their hundreds feared that the crew would meet certain death and the pier be badly damaged. Miraculously the barque struck the pier near its entrance. Ropes were thrown, the crew scrambled ashore and Blackpool's publicity officer telegraphed around the country to bring in sightseers. Three shops on the pier were destroyed by the impact, much of their stock falling into the sea, which attracted local people. Sodden furs and cheap jewellery were retrieved, illegally, from the waves as soon as it was safe to approach. For months, the search for *Sirene* plunder absorbed hopeful trippers.

Talbot Square, Blackpool, 1908. It was thronged throughout the holiday season. From here visitors could board trams or wagonettes to take them to strawberry gardens and village inns throughout The Fylde. Talbot Road, leading to the new station which had opened in 1898, was thick with new arrivals. The ornamental wrought-iron drinking fountain with its weather cock aloft was a favourite meeting place for locals and visitors alike, but as traffic and crowds continued to increase, it had to go.

Aviation Week, 18–23 October 1909, drew 20,000 people to the ground, with large numbers each day despite wet weather towards the end of the events. The Blackpool Tower Company offered a prize to the first British aviator who piloted an all-British machine and covered 100 yards without touching the ground. It was, however, the French aviators, notably M. Rougier who managed to remain in the air half an hour, who won the day. Lancashire's own A.V. Roe travelled 100 yards but never took off. He decided his propellors were too large.

Coronation celebrations, June 1953. Countless trippers arrived at the excursion platforms at Blackpool, including this crowd of workers from the Bury Felt Factory.

North Pier, Blackpool, 1920s. Two pleasure boats, *Wellington* and *Bickerstaffe*, are anchored off the pier. They conveyed hundreds of visitors to Southport, North Wales and Morecambe besides doing trips around Morecambe Bay. The spacious sun lounge at the pier head was a further attraction.

Talbot Square, Blackpool, 1911. In the centre is Yates's Wine Lodge, and thirteen heraldic beasts on columns surround the square, possibly erected as part of the celebrations for the Coronation of King George V.

Princess Parade looking south, August 1913. This world-famous promenade stretched 3 miles from North Pier to Victoria Pier. In the form of terraced esplanades at North Shore, it also featured a tramway, carriage drive and sea wall.

Blackpool central beach and Tower early this century. Raphael Tuck's postcard mirrors essential Blackpool: the gigantic wheel, the Tower, sailing boats, paddling and the inevitable huge crowds at Britain's most popular seaside resort.

Blackpool Tower ballroom, August 1907. On 14 December 1956 the Tower ballroom and lounge were destroyed by fire caused by a smouldering cigarette. Forty tons of scaffolding, 1,000 gallons of paint and 6,750 books of gold leaf were used in the restoration which took eighteen months and cost £5 million.

The Tower, Cenotaph and old Metropole, 1977. Blackpool Tower is dressed up with flags and bunting to celebrate Queen Elizabeth II's Jubilee. During the Second World War the resort was even more popular in other ways, with visitors, evacuees and RAF service personnel waiting to be drafted abroad. Many important records together with civil service staff to administer them were housed at Blackpool. Everyone benefited from a stay by the sea. The ever-popular Blackpool rock was introduced by Ben Bullock, a sugar boiler, after his stay at the house of John Pilling, sub-postmaster in Talbot Road. His first consignment, with 'Blackpool' lettered through the sticks, was sold out in a few hours. Mr Bullock retired to Southport where he died in 1905. On her recent visit, in 1994, the Queen was presented with a stick of Blackpool rock measuring 3ft.

Roof-top view, Blackpool, 1960s. The town was packed with visitors winter and summer alike. Blackpool Illuminations in the autumn and talented shows (often tried out in Blackpool before opening in the West End of London) extended the holiday season considerably. The glass dome of the Winter Gardens can be seen, as can the white Woolworths building, dwarfed only by Blackpool Tower itself, 500 ft high. Serried ranks of houses and expanding industry – all are evident.

St John's Church in Talbot Road, the tower of which was perhaps one of the few buildings to remain unchanged, rises in the centre of this view. It is interesting to note that the most ancient object in all Blackpool, an ice-age erratic boulder washed from the clay cliffs more than a century ago, is preserved outside St John's. Another one, at Norbreck, has been made into a sun dial.

Hornby Road, Blackpool, 1959. Stella, with mother Catherine Rothwell, has come into Blackpool for a day's shopping. Their favourite rendezvous is R.H.O. Hill's department store, which in later years was destroyed by fire. Hornby Road was a street full of reasonably priced boarding houses and shops selling buckets, spades and rock. Here the archetypal, good-natured landlady cared for guests with old-fashioned Lancashire hospitality. The most select shopping area thirty years ago was in Queen's Street but recession and the building of Hounds Hill Centre have turned this into a ghost of its former self.

Stanley Park, Blackpool, late 1960s. In the distance is the band stand. The park was opened by the 17th Earl of Derby in 1925 and consisted of an extensive area of gardens, bowling greens, lake, etc. When the park was laid out, during the years of the Depression, it provided employment for hundreds of local men.

Blackpool Police Station, South King Street, 1960s. The first police station for the borough force, which was established in 1887, used a building in Abingdon Street. By 1891 this was inadequate as the population had risen to 23,840. On 5 June 1895 the South King Street premises were opened by Mayor Alderman James Cardwell, using a golden key. There was a courtroom, garage and parade ground and Mr Durham, the Chief Constable, lived on the premises. This building has been replaced by new premises which opened in 1974.

New Promenade South Shore, Blackpool, *c*. 1900. The Pleasure Beach Big Dipper, much motorised traffic and overhead tram cables have not yet arrived. On the right some of the long gardens by the Headlands Private Hotel still remain.

Rough sea, Blackpool South Shore promenade, 1968. South Pier is in the background. Storms in 1977 flooded houses and did much damage all along the Fylde coast as far as Morecambe and beyond.

Singleton Thorpe, 1914. Tradition says that an immense inrush of seas in 1555 swept away the village of Singleton Thorpe; the inhabitants fled for their lives. Those escaping the waves set up a new village inland. Singleton Church is in the background as school children have a gardening lesson. The boys dig and the girls hoe.

Larbreck Hall, 1908. Once a moated house, the hall is situated near Poulton-le-Fylde. Here teas were served for travellers on their way to Blackpool.

A men's outing to the coast, *c.* 1920. They are lined up outside the Miller's Arms where Charles J. Pearson was licensee. It may have been Singleton Gala time as there is a merry-go-round pitched in the inn yard.

Singleton Service Station, *c.* 1900. 'Agricultural Engineers, Shoeing and General Smiths' is still to the fore in this rural community, as is the wheelwright's shop next door. When motor cars appeared this was a regular calling place for petrol en route to Blackpool or on the return journey to East Lancashire.

The Fylde coast fire fighters, *c.* 1900. These men, based at Singleton, frequently dealt with fires in thatch or haystacks which could ignite by spontaneous combustion. At first all that could be relied upon was a manual engine with a big water tub usually filled from streams and ponds.

July 1913. Jewsbury and Brown's 'lurry' has skidded off the road into a ditch. The mineral water manufacturing business at Lower Green, Poulton-le-Fylde made frequent deliveries to Blackpool and other coastal resorts and was very busy in the season supplying the piers and inns.

Wardleys, River Wyre, *c.* 1917. Ships sailed from this ancient port to the Baltic and Russia; trade was inaugurated by the Kirkham flax weaving merchants Messrs Langton and Birley. Warehouses, built in 1825 but now gone, can be seen in the background. Emigrants sailed from Wardleys on the *Six Sisters*, taking their own food supplies.

Skippool, River Wyre, *c.* 1920. In the seventeenth century Skippool was a favourite haunt for cock-fighting. William Blackburn of Thistleton and Messrs Hankinson and Hornby traded with the West Indies, and some owners of vessels registered at Poulton were involved in the slave trade.

Shard Bridge, River Wyre, *c.* 1900. The bridge was built in 1864 on the site of the original ferry crossing run by the Thompson family. Matthew Bamber collected tolls for the Shard Bridge Company and his wife made and sold Wardleys toffee.

The Breck, Poulton-le-Fylde, 1870s. The Breck led to the ports of Skippool and Wardleys. The sign of the Ship Inn above the three men and a dog indicated the sea-faring nature of the town in those days. 'Breck' means a gently sloping hill and is of Norwegian origin.

Maria Danson, née Rawcliffe, with her grand-daughter Anna Maria, *c.* 1906. The family bible records that, on 12 May 1877, Maria married James Danson. Over the next nineteen years she had nine sons followed by her only daughter, Jennie, born 24 December 1896. James died two years later; Maria on 22 November 1919 at the age of sixty. She is buried in Moorland Road Cemetery, Poulton-le-Fylde. Maria had extensive Fylde Coast connections, but it is her family history that is particularly interesting. Her dark good looks are thought to be of Spanish origin. When a Spanish ship was wrecked off Rossall officers were taken prisoner but the sailors were left to fend for themselves. They survived only because Fylde country people, out of pity, took them into their farms and cottages. Subsequently some married into the local community.

Marsh Mill, near Blackpool, 1920s. T. Kirkham's smithy, the drying house and the mill cottage were still standing. The mill was built by Bold Fleetwood Hesketh in 1794. He employed the famous millwright Ralph Slater. In the sixteenth century there were forty peg or post mills in The Fylde, an area which became known as Windmill Land. Tenants had to use the Lord of the Manor's mill to grind their corn and the miller collected his payments in kind, in a multure bowl. By 1900 the demand was for a fine, white flour so Marsh Mill only ground meal for farm use. In the 1930s the mill became a café but, after recent restoration, is now the focal point of a shopping complex and is the only remaining working mill.

Saturday 1 July 1893. The 11 p.m. holiday special train from Blackpool, travelling too fast, came off the track at Poulton Curve. The engine, in tearing up the permanent way, ploughed through an embankment and, crossing the main track, set fire to the guard's van. Driver Cornelius Ridgway and three passengers were killed.

Bertha Wyatt, 1901. With friends from The Fylde Seagull Cycling Club, in 1901, Bertha Wyatt toured the Lancashire coast as far as Grange-over-Sands, calling at the then many 'Cyclists' Rest' inns along a route now known as the Coastal Way.

William Smith's Motor Service, early 1900s. It ran from Market Square, Poulton, to the coast, calling at Carleton, Bispham, etc. Advertisements like '6d. Blackpool Tower, Famous Pleasure Resort, Circus, Great New Programme' helped to fill the bus.

The Festival Jazzmen, 1970s. Left to right: Pete Holden, Derek Aitkens, Cyril Wroe, Mike Lunn, Adrian Ridgway, Gerry Gerone. Seated: Bill Scott. Along with the Fylde Coast Jazzmen, the Wyre Levee Stompers and the Jazz Aces these local musicians performed at venues along the Fylde coast and beyond.

The road to Windy Harbour, early 1900s. Lonely and unfrequented, the harbour was on the River Wyre beyond Shard Bridge. Nowadays a large caravan park, popular with holidaymakers, spreads along the river bank.

Thorn tree, near Risecar Farm. In the 1930s sea winds blowing from Bispham caused this old tree to bend and re-root itself. Risecar Farm, like Rington, had stone walls made from seashore cobbles. In documents, name changes for this centuries-old site include Ryescarre, Risecar and Riseka.

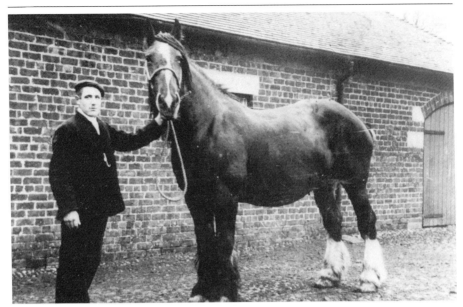

Farm horse with an agricultural labourer on a Bispham farm, *c.* 1903. The farm may be Knowle Farm which, in the seventeenth century, was the Singleton family country house. In an area well known for horse pasture, gravel was moved from the beach by horse and cart to assist with road building (see page 76). This was stopped as it accelerated coast erosion.

Edmund Freeborn and his family, *c.* 1890. He looked after Marsh Mill and had eight children, four boys and four girls. Two of the sons, Robert and William, helped by chaining the sacks together on the bottom floor and hauling them through trap doors to the dust floor at the top of the mill (see page 62).

Manchester Mercury

May 31st, 1785

"Cleeveleys, near Blackpool, John Salthouse respectfully acquaints the public that he has taken and genteely fitted up the Inn or Bathing House called Cleeveleys. Last year in the possession of Anthony Salthouse, and that he hopes by proper attention, a disposition to please, and good accomodation of all kinds, to merit the patronage and support of the ladies and gentlemen who may please to favour this coast with their company."

Advertisement, *Manchester Mercury*, 1785. Even this early visitors were encouraged to stay at Cleeveleys Bathing House and Bishop Pocock referred to sea-bathing at Blackpool in 1750. The railway did not arrive until 1840. Since 1838 there had been a daily conveyance at Poulton which met The Fylde Union Coach. It carried passengers to and from the new bathing station at Fleetwood every morning and evening during the season. There was sea-bathing also at Rossall, and a mansion 'situate at New Bispham near the sea-shore, two miles from Rossall Hall' was let for the summer season.

Cleveleys station, Thornton, *c.* 1900. The first station, 'Ramper', closed in 1843 but, in 1865, 'Cleveleys' was opened near this site. On 1 April 1905 the name was again changed to 'Thornton for Cleveleys'. By the 1920s, when it had become 'Thornton Cleveleys', crowds five deep lined the platform during the holiday season.

The bathing grounds, Cleveleys, 1920s. Cleveleys Hydro is in the background. The Hydro was fully licensed, heated throughout and possessed hydropathic baths, an eighteen-hole golf course, tennis courts and a resident orchestra in a Palm Court setting. The large area it covered is now packed with houses and bungalows.

Garden party, Cleveleys Hydro, 1911. It was described as the Hydro of the summer and winter resort. The driving force behind much coastal expansion was civil engineer B.C. Sykes whose Eryngo Lodge had been transformed into Cleveleys Hydro by 1902.

Dutch Cottage, 1906. This was one of fifty entries in the Cleveleys Garden City Exhibition supported by Sir Edwin Lutyens. In 1908 the Homesteads and Small Holdings Exhibition was held at Rossall Beach. Larkholme Estate Garden City was projected in 1931. Such endeavours all rose from Sir Peter Hesketh Fleetwood's dream of town dwellers owning seaside properties.

Norbreck Hydro, 1970s. By this time it had been transformed by James H. Shorrocks and greatly expanded from Norbreck Villa, which had been leased to him at the turn of the century. He built another storey topped with battlements which led to the name Norbreck Castle. He probably copied the idea from the two battlemented gazebos at Rossall Hall. Sewerage work and the making of Queen's Drive, and, later, the Gynn Estate Company's King's Drive, were further improvements which helped to attract more visitors to this seaside mecca perched on the cliffs and renowned for wonderful sea air.

A hundred years ago Norbreck and Bispham villages consisted of a cluster of cottages or 'biggins' made from puddled clay plastered on wattles with thatched roofs supported by crucks. A soot loft ran along the chimney and there was a canopy over the hearth. Outside, by the door, a 'speere' or draught protector was erected and sometimes a small porch against which leaned the turf stack. Fishing, shrimping and cockling were the mainstay of the cottagers. Communities complete with blacksmith and wheelwright and the occasional tinker, pedlar or delivery cart from Poulton or Fleetwood were almost self-supporting. The rising majesty of Norbreck Castle Hydro must have been an eye-opener for the natives.

FLEETWOOD TO
SUNDERLAND POINT

Rough sea, Morecambe, c. 1910.

Sea wall, Rossall, 1953. Breached by heavy seas, it was a reminder of what occurred in 1927 when the town of Fleetwood was engulfed and cut off for three days. On 29 July 1927 the Fleetwood Urban District Council Act received royal assent giving powers to construct and maintain adequate sea defences, but 28 October of that year brought disastrous flooding before the sea wall could be built. Throughout history high incursions of the Irish Sea have occurred at roughly fifty-year intervals. The Lords of Rossall retreated across the river to Hackensall Hall when this happened.

Storms, cyclones and water spouts had all been reported, delaying Her Majesty's mails. Iron steamships like the *Duke of Argyle* usually triumphed, but one early casualty was the Lancashire Steam Navigation Company paddle steamer *Her Majesty*. She sank in 1849, only five years after she had been placed on the Fleetwood to Belfast run.

Wyre Fishermen's Co-operative Society Ltd, Adelaide Street, near Fleetwood Market, 1970s. The premises are for sale. Following the result of the Cod War the society was forced to wind up, as was the Fleetwood Fishing Vessel Owners' Association who, as early as the 1920s, had been alarmed at the depletion of fish stocks. The association organised exploratory trips into other waters, notably the voyage by the *Florence Brierley* which sailed from Fleetwood on 22 March 1927. Faced by the vacuum-like sweeping of the sea bed by other countries, and lack of government support, the association inevitably succumbed. 'No fishing can hope to flourish which depends on the catching of immature fish' warned scientist C.F. Hickling on the *Florence Brierley* expedition.

Belgian trawler crew, Fleetwood, 1943. They had been fishing off Iceland. Their selling agent in the fishing port was Mr Friswell. According to international commercial law, Armement Ostendais under its manager Anton Van Beirs had the right to represent the firm in another country provided they had three administrators. In 1940 this Belgian trawler firm used their fleet to escape when Hitler over-ran France and Belgium. Many of their trawlers, when they arrived at Fleetwood, were requisitioned for mine sweeping, but three remaining vessels, of which *Edouard Anseele* was one, were taken to sea by the crews in turn.

Crystal, 1900. She ran pleasure trips up the River Wyre. The Fleetwood Steam Pleasure Boat Company also offered 'grand river excursions to Wardleys and Wyre Lighthouse' on *Pioneer* and *Lune*, sailing daily from 10 a.m. until dusk. Judge Edward Abbott Parry's book *Butterscotia*, published in 1899, mentions this.

Funeral landaus, *c.* 1900. These horse-drawn landaus were part of the funeral service provided by J.W. Wilson and Sons in Fleetwood around the turn of the century. Moving with the times, they later used motor cars.

Prestonian, Preesall Jetty, 1920s. The 1,650-ton ship is loading rock salt. This fine, white, flocculent variety of salt was shipped as far as India. It was mined in the district of Over Wyre until discontinued because of subsidence.

The ferry boat *Wyresdale* leaves Fleetwood for Knott End, 1900. Other boats sailing at fifteen-minute intervals from this 1897-built landing stage were *Onward*, *Play Fair*, *Guarantee* and *Pilling*. To the left is the wooden slade from which the river pleasure boats sailed.

Fleetwood and Knott End Motors charabanc, 1920s. Enjoying a trip down the Fylde coast is John William Parrish, born 9 March 1876. Fourth from the right at the back, his wife Alice stands beside him. They married on 28 November 1900. He was chief engineer on a gentleman's yacht based at Fleetwood.

Fleetwood Urban District Council's traction engine, 1898. The driver is J. Cardwell. Built in 1888, by Thomas Green of Leeds (works number 1352), it was used in road-making for crushing gravel aggregate from Fleetwood beach (see page 66).

A deputation from Newfoundland under Prime Minister Sir Edward Maris at Wyre Dock, 22 March 1911 with a sailing grain ship and the Fleetwood grain elevator behind. When this was built, in 1882, to deal with increased grain imports, the Lancashire & Yorkshire Railway ordered the latest equipment to be provided. A ship's leg conveyed cargo from the hold on to a conveyor belt where it travelled a distance underground eventually to reach the top of the building. Shakers and blowers restored damaged grain before transferring it to storage silos, 143 of which were available. Four-masted barques brought the wheat: *Adelaide*, a German vessel, could carry 4,700 tons; the first iron barque *Candida* brought 1,600 tons. High expectations were disappointed however, and the elevator was such a prominent landmark it had to be destroyed at the beginning of the Second World War. Officials in this group are Councillor R. Crookall, R. Jackson (British Trawlers Federation), Mayor James Robertson, C. Nicoll (Fleetwood Fishing Vessel Owners' Association) and C.F. Hickling (scientific adviser).

Captain Jack Ronan's seafaring career spans 50 years, of which 40 were with the Isle of Man Steam Packet Company. In 1945 when wartime Fleetwood was the main port serving the Isle of Man he was a junior rating on the 1905-built *Mona's Isle IV*. Gaining his mate's certificate in 1957, he progressed to become chief officer under Captain Lyndhurst Callow, master of the magnificent *Lady of Mann*. The *Lady*, as she was affectionately known, was purpose-built for the flourishing Fleetwood trade.

On promotion to captain in 1970 Captain Ronan was to command every vessel in the company fleet and as master professionally visited the Lancashire ports of Liverpool, Preston, Fleetwood, Heysham, Barrow and Manchester dry dock, but was mostly in command of the *Ben My Chree* V. He also held the river pilot's licence for all the principal ports.

It was the end of an era when sailings from Fleetwood to the Isle of Man ceased in 1961. On the evening of 11 September when *Mona's Isle V*, the last ship to leave Fleetwood, headed for Barrow for her winter lay-up, Captain Ronan was her second mate. Also on board was one of his longstanding friends, Ronnie Jackson of Knott End, an authority on Isle of Man Steam Packet Company ships. Happily, sailings were restored in 1971 and Captain Ronan was one of the first masters in command coming up the Wyre Channel. Such was the continuity of the company and its personnel, he also commanded the *Mona's Isle*, purchased for the ro-ro service to Heysham in 1985.

On retirement, Captain Ronan, a native Manxman of Castletown, accepted a relieving position with the Fisheries Office of the Isle of Man Government. After 50 years he is proud to have kept his Fylde links and refers to the people of North Lancashire as the salt of the earth.

Paddle steamer *Waverley*, 1977. The oldest paddle-steamer still in service, she visited the Lancashire coast in 1977, picking up passengers at Fleetwood. Launched in 1946, she replaced a ship sunk in 1940 returning with troops from Dunkirk. She belongs to the Paddle Steamer Preservation Society and is presently due for a £350,000 re-fit.

Stella Marina, 1960s. This white Norwegian vessel made trips from Fleetwood to the Isle of Man in the 1960s. Because of her shallow draught rough seas made for uncomfortable crossings, so she did not remain long in service.

Stella Marie, off Fleetwood, 5 October 1941. The Faroese schooner was anchored 4 miles out when worsening weather caused her cable and anchor to part. The lifeboat was launched into heavy seas; the rescue was a dangerous one. The eight-man crew of the schooner spent a day and night, first on deck and later in the rigging, in seas of terrific violence. Lifeboat Coxswain Jeff Wright reported that his craft was continually submerged and hurled against the stricken schooner, causing the steel pintle of the lifeboat rudder to jam. Jeff and the mechanic Sid Hill were both awarded RNLI silver medals for their part in the rescue which saved every man of the ship's crew. *Stella Marie* was one of the last sailing ships on the Lancashire coast.

Paul Rothwell, Santa Fé Express, Fleetwood, 1975. Language student and Fleetwood resident, he drove the miniature train in the summers of 1975 and 1976. Owned by Fleetwood Pier Company the train ran from near the pier, along the front, to a terminus at Beach Road. In later years the train was sold to a firm in Aberdeen. The track is now buried under blown sand as though the little railway, which gave so much pleasure to hundreds of children and adults, never existed.

The last major fish auction, Wyre Dock, 1979. By this year the landings had fallen to 18,000 tons from 34,000 tons in 1975. Sad faces reflect the virtual end of a great fishing port. Ironically, some years later, Icelandic vessels with their catches were welcomed at Wyre Dock by MP Sir Walter Clegg. Auctions took place again, but these were short-lived, and occurred only in May, July and August 1985.

In 1841 the Fleetwood Fishing Company was founded. It grew from a fleet of six fishing smacks at a time when fishermen had no thought of auctions. Small-masted sailing boats were used to catch a few stones of fish and returned rapidly to sell in the town or from the beach. In those early days fishing was in the hands of two familes: the Wrights from Marshside and the Leadbetters from Banks. Four men sorted out sales: Richard Leadbetter, John Johnson, William Holden, Richard Ashcroft. Harry Melling organised the first fish auction.

Singletons, boat builders, were founded in 1842. On deposit of £100 the shipmaster would supply a boat at once, the remainder being paid in quarterly instalments. By 1870 eighty-four sloops were operating but the method of boat purchasing and fish landing had altered. Larger boats with trawl beams and hand winches in the bows were used, until the arrival of the first steam trawlers, which could catch four times more than the sailing smacks.

Royalist, FD24, 1960s. She was the last of the deep-sea trawlers which cast their nets over the side of the vessel. They were replaced by stern trawlers. Fleetwood's top-earning trawler for 1960 was the 426-ton *Ssafa* which grounded on rocks off the island of Coll, Argyllshire in the same year.

Jacinta, FD159, 1960. One of the best known of Marr's stern trawlers, she heads for Wyre Dock after a trip in Icelandic waters. A previous *Jacinta*, FD 21, built in 1955, was owned by the Dinas Steam Trawling Co. Ltd (later taken over by Marr's). An even earlier *Jacinta* figured in the 1940 Dunkirk evacuation, Operation Dynamo, under Lieutenant E.J. Jordan.

Thomas Hodgkinson and his wife seated outside their cottage, Staynall, 1898. Visitors to the Fylde coast travelled the Over Wyre district in wagonettes or by the Garstang and Knott End Railway. The Hodgkinsons would have known Ben Alty, the peat cutter, who brought in a cart his dried turves for burning in the cottages. Another caller was Sabina Gallagher, water-cress gatherer, who sucked a clay pipe. William Percy of Stakepool lived in an old bathing van which he trundled from place to place. There were other characters: Adam Houghton of Rose Cottage, Damside, born on 8 March 1816, covered hundreds of miles on foot as a local preacher and lived until he was ninety. These country people lived long and healthily. Harry Hodgkinson, grandson of Thomas, walked from Charing Cross, London to Damascus Gate, Jerusalem in 1936 and became an authority on the Balkans.

Peggy Isles (now Peggy Stirzaker) and friend, Sunnyhurst Farm, Old Tom's Lane, Stalmine, c. 1924. Scholars of Stalmine British School, they feed the hens. To this day the farm supplies free-range eggs. Wagonette parties used Stalmine as a stopping-off place for strawberry teas. For over one hundred years Stalmine post office was run by the Porter family. Originally it was part of the Seven Stars Inn next to the church which has seven stars painted above the chancel. There was plenty of business for two inns but, once the motor age arrived, Catterall & Swarbrick took the licence away from the old Pack Horse Inn opposite the Seven Stars. The Porters therefore decided to turn the Pack Horse Inn into a post office, using the old inn bar as a counter.

The windmill, Pilling, 1959. Designed by Ralph Slater, the well-known millwright, and built near the remains of the old water mill by the Broadfleet river, it worked well. In 1886 a steam engine was installed and the sails taken down. The first mill on this site was erected in 1232.

Broadfleet Bridge, 17 July 1940. The stonework is reputed to bear the hoofmark of the devil. Wood from the sails of the mill by the river was made into gateposts and furniture. Eventually the windmill was converted into a private dwelling.

Cottages, Pilling Moss, 1900. The road on which the village children stand is 'springy to travel on' as it is raised above peat-cutting beds. By 1836 black-headed gulls were established on the Moss. Nightly raids were made to steal eggs, which troubled 'Old Kay' the watchman.

The old church, Pilling, 1960. Now opened only occasionally, it has an ancient font. A sundial above the door is in memory of Reverend George Holden who was appointed vicar on 11 May 1758. He was a brilliant mathematician who compiled tide tables used at Liverpool.

King Orry IV stranded on Thurnham Marshes, January 1976. Sold to R. Taylor of Bury for breaking up at Glasson Dock, she drifted up the Lune Estuary and grounded in a severe north-westerly storm. She remained high and dry until the next spring tides.

Cockersand Moss, 1960. The metal lighthouse stands where one of the first beacons on the coast was lit, by monks of Cockersand Abbey 800 years ago. So wild was the sea, the bones of dead monks were washed from their graves in the abbey burial ground.

Ox roast, Market Square, Lancaster, 9 August 1902. This was to honour the coronation of King Edward VII. Lancaster also held the mayor's annual venison feast, the buck, from the Forest of Bowland, being presented by Lord Cavendish.

Registered lodging houses for seamen, China Lane, Lancaster, 1880s. The Lord Nelson was situated near here. Some old inns, originally gentlemen's houses, received visitors. HRH Prince William of Gloucester stayed at the King's Arms on 21 September 1803.

Lancaster Castle, 1902. Henry V and King John built parts of the fortification but, by the sixteenth century, it was in need of repair. The early fifteenth-century gateway is named after John of Gaunt, Duke of Lancaster, although the duke did not visit more than twice.

A Lancaster-registered yacht, 36 LR, River Lune, *c.* 1900. She might have been built at Glasson Dock, where building of small vessels continued into the twentieth century. Lancaster was not a suitable position for the construction of large ships and the Lancaster Shipowners' Company went into liquidation with huge debts in 1869.

New Docks, Heysham, *c.* 1930. The new port was important as a terminal for Irish traffic. In 1904 it took 2,000 workmen seven years to complete the deep-water harbour, at a cost of over £3 million. Twenty locomotives and an army of Irish navvies were needed for the excavation, the workers being housed in 'Dawson City' and 'Klondyke' by contractors Price and Willis.

St Patrick's chapel, 1960. This early Saxon chapel was dedicated to St Patrick who, according to legend, was intent on bringing Christianity to the Lancashire Coast and was wrecked in Morecambe Bay. The chapel, one of the most ancient in the country, has walls 2½ ft thick, bonded by mortar thought to have been made by burning sea shells.

Heysham Headland. There are six ancient graves hewn out of rock close to the chapel of St Patrick. He is said to have landed here after crossing the Irish Sea on a millstone. In a hollow, a short distance away, is the thicket of trees, bent by sea winds, which is thought to have once been a druid grove.

'Don't obstruct the traffic at Morecambe', 1930s. The popular picture postcard illustrates both fairground and carnival spirit on the Lancashire coast. At Blackpool, Fleetwood and Morecambe carnivals and beauty queen competitions were highlights of every summer season.

Heysham, 1903. Nettle beer was sold and teas made for visitors at a time when every cottage advertised the sale of herb beer. Mrs Kellett looks out from premises dated 1633. The name of this ancient village is said to derive from the 'ham' or home of chieftain Hesse.

'A few lines from Morecambe' was a popular card in the 1930s and is now quite valuable as a collector's item: the postman's bag opens to show ten views of the resort. Among these is the Flagstaff area congregated with deck chairs and from where trips to Morecambe Bay Holiday Camp and the new promenade slopes at Heysham were made. From the Slade boat trips were made into Morecambe Bay, running all day long in season. From Harbour Garage in the 1930s Silver Grey luxury coaches took visitors into the Lake District. The last Lancaster-built sailing ship, launched at Glasson Dock in January 1887, ended her career at Morecambe after featuring in films and serving as the show ship Moby Dick. She was burned out in 1970. Also shown in the postman's bag was the busy Midland Hotel, then quite new. It has since been used as a set for a Hercule Poirot film. Dancing and skating were available at the Empress Hall, while the Winter Gardens at West End, owned by theatre managers W.H. Broadhead and Sons, featured numerous attractions.

A few lines from
Morecambe

Bathing pool, Bare, Morecambe, 1930s. Morecambe promenade stretched as far as Bare at the east end, which was laid out with rock gardens and walks. A fine clock tower was presented by John Robert Birkett who was mayor from 1903 to 1906. The Channings was the largest hotel in this obviously popular area.

Donkeys on the sands, Morecambe, 1908. The steamer in the background may be going to Blackpool or Southport.

Central promenade, Morecambe, July 1935. In view are the bandstand, flagstaff, Winter Gardens (behind the bandstand), the old stone pier and the gardens near Central Pier. To the left some wagonettes are still available although the motor car has made its appearance.

Morecambe, *c.* 1890. The thriving seaside resort featured in a round the coast survey in the nineteenth century. Almost as popular as at Blackpool, the piers were thronged, landaus and horse-drawn trams plied for trade and there were tricycles for hire (right). The lady in the foreground has an oyster stall.

Number One Troupe, entertainers, West End, Morecambe, 1910. Concerts, skating, dancing and The Tower built in an Eastern style of architecture were once the town's main attractions. Sea bathing was popular as far back as 1820 when Poulton-le-Sands was a village of 400 people.

Central Pier, Morecambe, 1916. The Central Pier has a fine pavilion and free roof garden at the end. The Ideals concert party was giving performances that season and there was 'dancing daily'.

First Terrace, Sunderland Point, *c.* 1930. For centuries, as at Glasson, haaf draught and drift net fishing was carried on, as was 'whammeling' which used a 300-yd drift net. The Gardner family, well-known River Lune pilots, went whammeling in lugsail-rigged boats. The haaf or lave net is a net bag attached to an 18-ft long pole supported by three legs. James Spencer of Sunderland Point, whose family did the job for 90 years, piloted vessels for 5s a journey.

Although Snatchem's Marsh, 2 miles of tidal road, cuts off Sunderland Point twice daily, it was once the port for Lancaster, with extensive West Indian and African trade. Vessels carrying gunpowder tied up by the Powder Stump at a safe distance. Glasson, with its safer anchorage, replaced Sunderland. The latter's best-known inhabitant has come down to us as Sambo, the little black boy who reputedly died of a broken heart when his master left. Sambo's grave is still visited and tended but it is more likely that he died of cholera, as Sunderland reported 'alarming accounts of the progress of cholera' in the eighteenth century.

Anglo-Norman doorway, Overton, c. 1960. Francis Raby, an Overton man, was the first keeper of Abbey Scar lighthouse, Cockersand and Plover Scar lighthouse. He was paid £25 a year for this job which remained in his family for generations. To augment his income he also made baskets for mussel gatherers. Cockersand Abbey stone probably went into the cottages of Overton whose inhabitants were supplied with spinning wheels to deal with American cotton landed at Sunderland Point.

Parish church of St Helen, Overton, 1950s. This church may be almost a thousand years old and the oldest in Lancashire. The bell was presented in January 1878 by W. James Thompson of Barrow. An Anglo-Norman doorway (see above), ornamented with beaked and chevron designs, dates from between 1050 and 1140.

River Lune, Halton Hall, Lancaster, 1908. In the 1890s the hall was the home of the Sharpe family. They went punt-gunning at low water on Arnside sands where grey geese rested after their 500-mile flights. The camouflaged punt floated slowly down channel and the tired geese were easy prey.

Morecambe Bay frozen, 1895. On Southport's Marine Lake there were ice floes and all along the coast fishing 'nobbies' and small boats were crushed in the ice of this phenomenal winter.

HEST BANK TO

BARROW

Promenade, Grange-over-Sands, 1916.

Hatlex Farm, Hest Bank, 1928. It was in the township of Slyne with Hest in 1866 when Hest was referred to as 'a small but pleasant bathing area on Morecombe Bay'. The Hest Bank Hotel was run by Jonathan Wilding, and Richard Wadeson was the stationmaster. Thomas Heaton and Sarah Knipe were the only farmers.

Hest Bank visitors early this century. A coach used to ply between Hest Bank and Ulverston 'as tide permitted'. In 1874 the high road over the sand to Leven, Kent and Ulverston was unique. Between the sixteenth and the nineteenth centuries more than 140 people were drowned, most of whom were buried at Cartmel.

Bolton-le-Sands, 1902. Visitors were photographed on the beach with a backdrop of the Lake District. A thick screen of trees protected the village from sea winds blowing off Morecambe Bay. Situated on salt marsh, it attracts wading birds before autumn migration.

Stankelt Road, Silverdale. This led to Jenny Brown's Point where an old lady of that name lived on the shore in the eighteenth century. It was once a place where copper smelting was carried on, the chimney stack at Crag Foot being a useful landmark for people crossing the sands.

Emesgate Lane, Silverdale, 1930s. In the centre is the fully licensed Royal Hotel where visitors stayed. Freshly caught Lune salmon was always on the menu.

The shore, Silverdale, early 1900s. Steamers from Morecambe Bay used to call here. The village was left high and dry in the 1920s when the River Kent changed course to reach the sea further westwards.

Castlebarrow, Silverdale, *c.* 1931. It is marked by a dungeon tower known as the Pepper Pot. This vantage point gives an excellent view over the plain, the Kent estuary and the sea.

Arnside Tower, in a dangerous condition, 1961. One of the chain of pele towers, it was burned down 'during a mightie winde' in 1602, but later rebuilt. Another great storm, in 1884, blew down one of its huge walls when the tide caused rivers to rise to a height previously unknown.

The beach, Arnside, July 1960. Over a century ago Arnside had a thriving salt trade. The sloop *Leighton* was specially built for carrying iron and slate. The Backbarrow Iron Company shipped a furnace to Arnside and among cargoes handled were hoops, marble, coal and gunpowder.

Arnside station, Furness Railway line, 1900. From here sea-washed turf, in demand for bowling greens, was despatched. In the late nineteenth century there were plans to enclose areas of salt marsh between Park Point, Arnside and Bolton-le-Sands.

Viaduct, Arnside Bay, 1923. The Ulverston and Lancaster Railway viaduct was constructed on the line of an old ford over the River Kent. Arnside was a fishing village where there was an important yacht and boat-building centre run by the Crosfield family.

Pier, Grange-over-Sands, *c*. 1910. Because of the tidal bore cargoes had to be unloaded quickly. 'Only at certain hours is the jetty accessible to steamboats that came from Morecambe' reports the 1895 round-the-coast survey; an 1849 directory describes it as 'covered one hour with ships, another with pedestrians'.

Ornamental Park, Grange-over-Sands, 1900. The gardens were laid out in the 1880s and became renowned: the many species of duck and wildfowl owned and managed by the Grange District Wildlife Association interest today's visitors. A spring from the sands, once the main water supply, persisted even after the gardens were made. 'Shortly after the tide receded the water was as pure again as though no salt had been near' (A.M. Wakefield). Benjamin Hall leased the land to Alexander Brogden for two years and, when the lease expired, Grange Council took over, finally buying the land in 1894. The name Grange-over-Sands is derived from the Augustinian monks of Cartmel Priory because they had their granary or 'grange' there.

Kent's Bank House, 1919. Overlooking the bay, it was a popular hotel which sent out cards advertising its grounds and public rooms. From Hest Bank to Kent's Bank is the 11-mile route of organised walks across Morecambe Bay now led by the official guide to the Kent sands, Cedric Robinson. In May 1985 Cedric accompanied the Duke of Edinburgh on an historic cross-bay carriage drive.

When the author Elizabeth Gaskell stayed at Lindeth Tower, Silverdale, she reported all sorts of people and types of conveyance making the crossing. Hest Bank was where the coaches started in the 1800s. Hest Bank Hotel was a posting house, once the Sands Inn, where a lantern was kept in an upper room for guiding travellers. At one time the steamer *Windermere* came up from Liverpool, off-loading hoops and wooden articles at Hest Bank.

Warning, Grange-over-Sands, 1960. Here a siren was sounded at the open-air swimming baths to alert people to leave the sands at once as the tidal bore came in with the speed of a cantering horse. Another warning gives the name and address of the official sand guide for any parties contemplating crossing the sands at low tide. At other places along the coast, for example Greenodd, there are similar cautions regarding quicksands and shoals.

DANGER
BEWARE
FAST RISING TIDES
QUICKSANDS
HIDDEN CHANNELS
SIREN WARNS OF INCOMING TIDE
IN EMERGENCY PHONE 999 AND ASK FOR COASTGUARD

Sailing, Grange-over-Sands, early 1900s. Grange was a popular yachting centre. The coal trade kept Grange busy in the sixteenth and seventeenth centuries but, with the coming of the railway in 1857, it grew into a genteel holiday resort.

Boarbank Hall, Allithwaite, 1918. It is reached by a side lane from Cark. In the nineteenth century, as soon as the tide turned, cockling carts from Allithwaite, Humphrey Head, Flookburgh, Cart Lane and Kent's Bank made for the open sea. The Guide Over the Sands Inn at Allithwaite has history in its name.

Steeplechase, Cartmel, 1930s. Two meetings a year are held, in spring and summer, lasting three and two days respectively. The spring bank holiday meeting draws huge crowds to this the smallest but most picturesque of the racecourses in Lancashire.

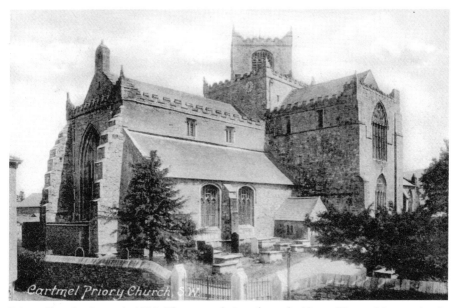

Priory Church, Cartmel, 1933. The name derives from the Norse 'Kartmeir', meaning 'a sandbank by a rocky ground'. Since the priory's foundation in 1188, the Augustinian canons remained in Cartmel for 400 years. Among other treasures found is an ancient chest which contained accounts and parish money. Three keys were needed to open it.

Old Joe, sexton and local character, 1903. Working above Morecambe Bay, he lived at Heversham and scythed the grass in churchyards. Here he is sharpening with carborundum the traditional blade which only an experienced man could wield. Walking the lanes, with his scythe over his shoulder, Joe much resembled Old Father Time.

In the early years of the century Constance Holme's minor classic *The Lonely Plough* was inspired by a tidal wave which covered the north of Morecambe Bay, Aldingham and Leighton Moss. Sweeping away an artificial tide barrier, the Lugg, it engulfed the Arnside-Heversham area. It resembled the storm in Edward I's reign which washed away the sixteenth-century church of Aldingham.

The ancient borough regalia of Flookburgh, 1905. It dates from the reign of Edward I. In 1890, when the cockling trade was at its height, 3,162 tons of cockles left the village of Flookburgh. The use of the 'Jumbo', a clumsy board which killed small fry, instead of the three-pronged 'cram', a less damaging instrument, threatened the trade, but the frost of 1895, in Morecambe Bay, killed thousands of these crustaceans. It became known as 'cocklers' foe' and led to much hardship.

The men who 'followed the sands' from Flookburgh, the principal fishing village, to Morecambe Bay now use tractors instead of horses and carts. In winter they used to mend their nets, finally dipping them in a bath of tar. Their simple cottages burned peat from Holker Moss, and in the corner of the peat house was a large iron pot for boiling shrimps.

'The Height', the Friends' Meeting House, 1908. It was built in 1677 and has a burial ground attached. In 1908 it had a female sexton who lived in the adjoining cottage. The chapel had a watch tower above the porch as the Quakers had to be alert to avoid rough handling by people who opposed them.

Arnside Viaduct, 1968. This 1,300-ft railway viaduct, built across the River Kent, carries the line from Carnforth to Barrow. When forty-six arches were driven 70 ft into the sand it was a Victorian engineering achievement, but it killed the shipping trade of Sandside, Milnthorpe and other small coastal ports.

The old Gateway, Cartmel, 1960. It is now a National Trust property. With the church this was all that was left of the priory buildings from the Augustinian priory dating from 1300. From 1624 to 1790 the building above the gateway served as a grammar school. Among many ancient and interesting relics at Cartmel Priory are copies of Spenser's *Faerie Queen* (1596), a 1502 black leather bible in six volumes and a folio copy of Foxe's *Book of Martyrs*. There is also an ancient umbrella, one of the first of its kind. Cartmel Priory, founded 1188, takes its name from 'Caer', a camp, and 'Meol', sand bank.

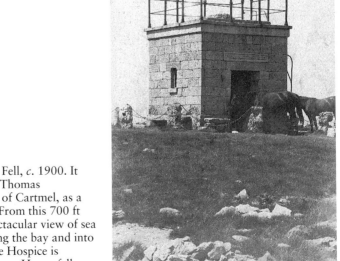

Hospice, Hampsfield Fell, *c.* 1900. It was built in 1834 by Thomas Remington, the vicar of Cartmel, as a refuge for travellers. From this 700 ft hill top there is a spectacular view of sea and peaks surrounding the bay and into the Lake District. The Hospice is universally referred to as Hampsfell.

Shrimping and cockling cart, Cark, 1929. The driver, Alfred Butler, was guide over the Leven estuary for over forty years. He was born in Allithwaite, where he learned from his forefathers the art of collecting flukes, cockles, mussels and shrimps and a vast knowledge of tides and shifting sandbanks.

Greenodd Station, early 1900s. In the nineteenth century Greenodd Harbour was busy handling iron ore from Furness. When the Furness Railway line was built through Grange-over-Sands and Ulverston a useful branch line was laid through Greenodd to the shores of Lake Windermere.

Ulverston, *c.* 1928. There are tricycles and street barrows selling vegetables, but few cars. In the eighteenth century it was a busy port. Market Square, cobbled with stones from the beach, became such a commercial centre that it was known as the 'Emporium of Furness', with regular hiring fairs and Thursday markets. Shifting sandbanks, a feature of this part of the Lancashire coast, eventually silted up the harbour. Shipping looked doomed until the 2-mile-long Ulverston Canal was built, in 1795, linking the town with the sea at Canal Foot. However, with the coming of the railway its days as a busy port were numbered, but the mail coaches northward still stopped here. At one time coaches could not resist the short but always hazardous trek across the sands of Morecambe Bay and some came to grief, blown over by high winds or caught by a surging tide. Even some cattle drovers with their herds of beasts from Scotland preferred to risk the 3 mile crossing from the north-east corner of Morecambe Bay near Kent's Bank, rather than take the longer, hillier route via Kendal.

Sir John Barrow's Monument, Ulverston, 1912. It is also known as the Hoad Monument because it is set on Hoad Hill. From the top of this lighthouse the view is magnificent. Sir John, who was born at Ulverston in 1764, was an explorer and Secretary to the Admiralty.

The town took its name from Ulpha, a Saxon chieftain; after the Norman Conquest the monks of Furness Abbey owned Ulverston. The Scottish raider Robert Bruce burned the town down twice.

La Argentina, 1939. Built by Vickers Armstrong, its masthead fitted with a Marconi aerial, this warship was undergoing trials under the direction of Lancashire coast man Fred Woods. Fred's father, T. Woods of 14 Albert Square, Fleetwood, printed the first edition of Porter's *History of The Fylde*. Fred had a passion for building aeroplanes made possible by his uncle, George Butler Woods, in his boat loft fitted with derricks. 'There were only two or three similar lunatics in the country in 1911 aiming at sustained flight without power', wrote Fred. He took his 30 ft sections of aeroplane over to Preesall on the ferry, for flying practice, where he created quite a stir. He later worked on direction finders for ships and became Development Engineer to Marconi Marine for merchant ships and the Marconi Wireless Company for Naval Work.

Bardsea, August 1923. At one time the route across the sands of Morecambe Bay ran all the way to Bardsea, near Ulverston, where the Ship Inn had a quay especially for the use of fishing and cockling men. Next to Baycliff and Bardsea is Aldingham which has lost more land to the sea than any place in the north-west.

Conishead Priory, north of Bardsea, 1932. It was founded in the twelfth century by Gamel de Pennington who liked the sea. This Gothic-revival building appeared in the 1820s: the original lake and grotto remain in the grounds. Later owned by a group of Tibetan Buddhist monks, in the 1930s it was a convalescent home for Durham miners.

Fisherman's Arms Hotel, Baycliff, 1930s. Situated on the west side of Morecambe Bay, on low banks out of the sea's reach, Baycliff attracted archaeologists as it was noted for its prehistoric stone circles.

Newbiggin Bay, Furness Coast Road, 1942. The Angles and Vikings who used this coast made roads which led to the thirteenth-century church at Urswick, where stained-glass windows may have come from Furness Abbey.

Furness Railway locomotive 0–6–0 Class D1 Number 18. It was built in 1871 and renumbered 24 in 1900. After useful service on the Furness Railway it was withdrawn in 1910. Involved in shipbuilding, and the manufacture of iron and steel, the railway also played a part in holiday developments.

Marshalling yards, Buccleuch Docks, Barrow-in-Furness, 1930. In the eighteenth century Barrow was an unremarkable village given up to sea bathing and the export of iron ore, malt, oats and barley. In forty years the Furness Railway transformed it from a hamlet to a steel town with a population of 60,000.

HRH Princess Mary launching HMS *Princess Royal*, Vickers Works, Barrow-in-Furness, early this century. The town's heraldic coat of arms showed a paddle steamer with the motto *Semper Sursum* beneath.

Launching of HIJMS *Kongo* by Madame Koike, Vickers Naval Construction Works, Barrow, 18 May 1912. She was destined for Japan.

Dreadnoughts, Devonshire Dock, Barrow-in-Furness, 1910. This railway-developed port, with 700 acres of water and quays, aimed for Liverpool standards. In 1868 a custom house was built. H.W. Schneider's and James Ramsden's efforts were reinforced by shipowners James Fisher & Sons. They built blast furnaces and eventually set up the Haematite Steel Company.

Walney Ferry, 3 August 1906. It plied between Barrow and Walney Island. Two years later this steam ferry was replaced by a bridge. In 1799 a lighthouse was erected on the southern tip of the island to supplement navigational aids at St Bee's Head and the Morecambe Bay lightship.

Swings, Biggar Bank, Walney Island, 1909. Walney is the largest of the Furness islands which protect Barrow. Smaller islands are Roa, Sheep and Piel, the last-named anciently known as the Pile of Fouldray. Flocks of seabirds now frequent the houses which were once homes of the pilots who brought boats up the Walney Channel. John Abel Smith, banker and chairman of the Tontine Company, which figured in the early years of Fleetwood's building, hoped to make a commercial success of Roa. He went as far as building a harbour for steamships, but his attempt failed as he over-reached himself.

On many occasions the tide has completely swamped Walney. During the fifteenth century, in an attempt to keep out the tide, Biggar Bank was built by the monks of Furness, whose abbot was accused of smuggling wool from Piel. Sand and gravel were unloaded at a small pier at Biggar Bank. According to tradition, at the time of the Armada a Spanish galleon, blown by storms, was wrecked and its timbers used in building the Queen's Head Inn.

Marchon Enterprise, on her maiden voyage, Whitehaven, 1962. By this time her sister ship *Marchon Venturer*, built at Wallsend, had already made 275 trips to Casablanca for cargoes of phosphate rock. Both ships, which carried scrap steel as well as phosphate rock, were managed by James Fisher on behalf of Albright & Wilson. When *Marchon Venturer* operated under general charter, flying the flag of the Annan Shipping Company, her skipper and eleven crew rejoined James Fisher and Company's pool of seamen at Barrow.

Barrow's large shipyard was building sailing vessels until 1934; the last was a four-masted steel barquentine for the Brazilian Navy; after this Vickers Armstrong Ltd took over the site. Daniel Brocklebank was the most famous of the Whitehaven shipbuilders. The yard operated from 1782 until its takeover in 1869 by the Whitehaven Shipbuilding Company.

Pack horse bridge, Broughton, 1898. Because of boundary changes parts of coastal Lancashire were lost to Cumberland and Westmorland. This ancient bridge is one example, photographed by the renowned Alfred Pettit.

Furness farmhouse, 1904. The interior reveals ancient oak beams, and original furniture handed down over the years. The massive farm tables, designed for use by the family and workers on the farm, were made in the kitchen and were too large ever to leave that room.

Furness Abbey Church, painted by Daniel Crosthwaite and engraved by F.W. Topham, *c.* 1830. It became a tourist haunt. The Cistercian monks chose the fertile 'valley of the deadly nightshade' as their place to build what became one of the richest and most powerful religious houses in England. It was founded in 1127 by Stephen, Earl of Morton and Boulogne. Little did the monks realise that centuries later the Furness Abbey Railway Station and the Furness Abbey Hotel, whose grounds adjoin the abbey itself, would hum with visitors to the famous sandstone ruins. In Burrow's one penny *Guide to Furness Abbey* the manager, H.P. Stephenson, informed readers that dinner at the hotel was one guinea and that the 'Abbot's room' had the 'celebrated bas reliefs made of marble and framed in black oak from the Abbey'.

Happy Valley Pierrots from Silloth, July 1904. 'Do you remember when we saw the pierrots in Allonby?' reads the message on this postcard. Like another popular troupe, The Jolly Tars, they moved along the Lancashire coast.

Late Victorian postcard, 1902. 'A cry from the deep', appropriate to northern Lancashire coastline, helped popularise the drama of turbulent seas in sea-bathing resorts. Visitors were particularly drawn by the lifeboat service and responded generously to appeals, such as that after the loss of the two lifeboat crews who went to rescue the *Mexico* in 1886.

Acknowledgements

Albright & Wilson Ltd • the late Vic Baldwin • Bamforths Ltd
the late George Barker • *Blackpool Gazette and Herald* • Norman Boyes
Stanley Butterworth • J. Colley • Mr. Danson • Bob Dobson
Susan Donaldson • The Festival Jazzmen • Derek Hawthornthwaite
the late Harry Hodgkinson • Denise Househam • the late Mr Innes
The Isle of Man Steam Packet Company • Joanna Isles
Lancashire Evening Post • Lancashire Record Office
Leeds and District Traction Engine Club • Norman Lund
Peter Martin, Associated British Ports, Fleetwood • Eric Mills
G. & R. Pemberton Ltd, Preston • Captain Jack E. Ronan
Sankeys of Barrow • Ron Severs • Ralph Smedley • Mrs L. Van Beirs
Richard West • Brian Williams

BRITAIN IN OLD PHOTOGRAPHS

To order any of these titles please telephone Littlehampton Book Services on 01903 721596